IMAGES
of England

AROUND BRIGG
THE SECOND SELECTION

A days sport in the Ancholme.

IMAGES
of England

AROUND BRIGG
THE SECOND SELECTION

John and Valerie Holland

TEMPUS

Mrs Allen's drapers shop at 6 Market Place, Brigg, specialised in baby linen, but, significantly. above the door is a large advertisement for Raphael Tuck & Sons, picture postcards. By 1906 when this photograph was taken, postcard collecting was becoming all the rage as the Edwardians filled their albums with a variety of subjects, from pretty greetings cards to local street scenes. They were bought from little shops like this, penny plain and twopence coloured, then posted to relatives and friends as the craze spread. The bubble burst at the end of the First World War, but postcard collecting is still pursued by enthusiasts today.

Frontispiece: The River Ancholme, flowing gently northward through Brigg to the River Humber, has always been a popular spot for fresh water fishing. This 1910 Brigg postcard shows the result of a day's fishing with this catch of bream and roach by the Drinkall brothers. Usually these types of fish would have been put back in the river, for the Ancholme was more famous for its eels and pike.

First published 2002

Tempus Publishing Limited
The Mill, Brimscombe Port,
Stroud, Gloucestershire, GL5 2QG

© John and Valerie Holland, 2002

The right of John and Valerie Holland to be identified as the Author of this work has been asserted by them in accordance with the Copyrights, Designs and Patents Act 1988.

British Library Cataloguing in Publication Data.
A catalogue record for this book is available from the British Library.

ISBN 0 7524 2641 9

Typesetting and origination by Tempus Publishing Limited
Printed in Great Britain by Midway Colour Print, Wiltshire

Contents

A *Lincolnshire Times* photographer captured members of St John's Church youth fellowship in a happy mood, at an informal concert held in the church hall, 1957. The authors are seated on the extreme right, front row, and standing fourth from the left, middle row.
(With copyright permission from the *Hull Daily Mail*).

Acknowledgements

Once again our thanks go to all the local people who have encouraged us to compile a second selection of old photographs of our area. Unfortunately it is impossible to name everyone individually who has helped us during the many years that have passed since our interest in the subject first began. During the last few months we have been touched by the number of people who have welcomed us into their homes, or visited ours, and given us their time. Without their generosity in both providing additional material and giving us the benefit of their local knowledge, our task would have been much more difficult. Special mention goes to Marjorie Thompson, Dorothy Todd, Nellie Reynolds, Mrs Cooper, Jim and Audrey Holland, Maurice Watson, George Green, Roy Leeson, Mike Hookham, John Goulby, Ken Braithwaite, Jack Taylor, Greta Burkinshaw, Irene Waby, Peter Gilbert, Philip Wood, Len and Betty Clark, John Beveridge, Walter and Edna Thorpe and Paddy O'Boyle. My sister, Christine Watkins typed the text. What would we do without her?

Valerie L. Holland

Introduction

It was a great pleasure to be asked to put together a further selection of old postcards and photographs from our collection relating to this part of North Lincolnshire. Since our first volume in this series, *Around Brigg*, was published in 1997 local people have shown us great interest and respect and straightaway were asking if we would compile a further selection of pictures. At the time, perhaps four years ago, it seemed a little premature to suggest that the public would want more. However, several things in the intervening years have led us to once again make the effort, particularly in the time required in getting to see necessary 'wise' locals, still older than us, both in our town and in the villages close by. Once the publishers had given us the final prod, Valerie and I were well motivated by the encouragement of our local history friends. It is all very well having a collection of postcards, pictures and ephemera, collected over almost half a life time, but such a collection needs the embellishment and intimate knowledge from the breadth of the local community. Luckily Valerie and I do know (and have known) the right people in the right villages and in our home town. Luckily they are the same folk that helped us in the past and they have encouraged us with their homespun friendliness and local knowledge that now accompanies and enhances these postcards and photographs in the form of captions.

Since 1997 our collecting has continued. Our search for postcards has taken us both far and near for the excitement of finding another unseen local view. We search the antique fairs, we comb the postcard specialist auctions and generally rely on dear friends throughout the country who share our hobby. Yes, it is a hobby but a much more expensive one than when we started collecting a quarter of a century ago. It seems that far more people now collect postcards and there are fewer of them to buy!

Several happenings since the first volume have encouraged us to compile a further one. In addition to words and letters received locally after the publication of *Around Brigg*, we have been forwarded correspondence by the publishers from varying parts of the world as well as from other regions of the United Kingdom. Even today some note may come through our letterbox asking for local information, or perhaps telling us some. It appears that our local history books can, and do, get posted far afield to distant Briggensians who still have pleasant memories of the area, especially when they see a collection of local images reminding them of the past, and perhaps, their youth.

Occasionally a letter arrives that seems trivial, but develops into a full-blown investigation. A writer from Saskatchewan in central Canada wanted local detailed help with her family tree, she was engrossed with her own studies but wanted more help. We gladly joined in her search and eventually sent her back a great deal of paper work. She was delighted and we were pleased.

A forty-minute phone call from Sydney, Australia, brought me in contact, one December morning, with a school friend who had left Brigg in 1967 for sunnier climes. This chiropractor felt very homesick having received our book as a Christmas present, 12,000 miles away. A month later a fat envelope of Brigg past and present was winging its way to the southern hemisphere – another happy day!

However, the most remarkable happening was the bringing together of two brothers, one in Leicester and one in Brigg, who had not met until recently and they didn't know each other even existed. The Brigg man was in his late eighties, the Leicester man about 60. Delving into family history brought the sixty-year-old to Brigg in search of possible brothers or sisters; he bought our book and scanned the pictures for family likenesses in crowd scenes and finally his patient wife sent us a letter asking for help. The challenge was accepted. Our local friends were contacted, older locals had their memories prodded, a hundred years of school records were perused and six months of effort was rewarded. Tears were shed when the two half-brothers came together in our presence. Perhaps this is another good reason to compile a further book of reminiscences. We had been surprised by the local interest shown in the book but even more surprised at this much wider interest – new friendships have resulted!

This volume does not follow quite the pattern of volume one. Firstly, our area around Brigg is brought into about a four or five mile radius, instead of the previous six. So four villages are not included this time, but it allows us to put in extra views of the remaining places. Secondly, in the main Brigg section we have put the postcards and photographs in time sections ranging from Victorian times, through pre-First World War times, between the two wars, through the Second World War up to about the time of the 1953 Coronation and then concluded with a selection of photographs of 'Vanishing Brigg', from the last twenty years or so.

Clearly times are changing. The postcards of the 'golden age' show a time when villages and small market towns were virtually self-contained with their own craftsmen and small shops and required very little outside help. That is not so now anywhere and the area around Brigg is no different. Gone are the wheelwrights, the blacksmiths, the farriers, and most of the village post offices, grocers and so on. Happily old postcards, if not too faded, can remind us of a completely different style of living when everyone at least appeared to be content with their lot. Perhaps this book will also bring a quiet smile of reminiscence to your face too.

One
Victorian Snippets

Picture postcards only became common at the beginning of the twentieth century, but this view of Brigg Market Place is of the year 1836, put onto a 1904 postcard. The main features of the cobbled market place are still recognisable on this engraving. The Buttercross is to the near left, with a horse and carriage outside the old Angel Hotel. Adjoining the Angel is the Lion Hotel. The newly built Ancholme Bridge is in the middle distance. The bulk of these folk are standing near the archway of Coney Court.

The Lion Hotel was in the Market Place and in direct competition with the Angel Hotel, especially as a posting house, illustrated on this billhead dated 1838. The Angel succeeded in attracting the lucrative coaching business, causing the Lion to cease trading by about 1860.

Chapel of St Mary. The construction of a small chapel of ease commenced in 1699 in Bigby Street. Built of red brick, it was mainly paid for by four gentlemen named Atkinson, Jolland, Benson and Dempster. A curate was appointed to read prayers daily and preach on Sundays as assistant to the vicar of Wrawby.

Brigg Church Lincolnshire.

The church of St John the Evangelist. When the old chapel became too small for Brigg's increasing population, a new church was built on the site in 1841/2. It was constructed of stone given by Sir John Nelthorpe, in the Gothic style at a cost of about £3,000. Lady Nelthorpe laid the first stone, 16 August 1841. William Cressey printed this engraving.

William Cressey, a printer and stationer, was appointed postmaster in 1846 and held the position for over fifty years. The post office illustrated here was in Wrawby Street, where his name can still be seen today on the yard sign by the side of the office.

The Market Place in the 1860s or early 70s. This very early photograph shows many differences from today in Wrawby Street and Bigby Street. William Coulson was a grocer and tallow chandler, whilst William Nainby (d. 1880) was an ironmonger and brazier. This building had been the Lion Hotel. Nainby's wife, Eliza, sold it to the Lincoln and Lindsey Bank in 1883.

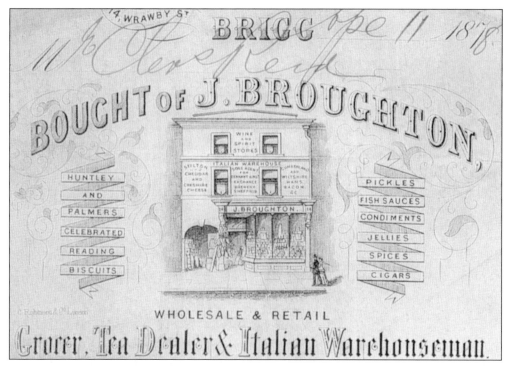

John Broughton, 14 Wrawby Street. This billhead of 1878 shows the wide range of goods stocked by a small grocery in a small market town. This delightful engraving probably serves to enhance the shop's actual exterior appearance. The family ran the business throughout the 1860s until into the 1890s. School Court looks much the same today.

In 1880 the Lincolnshire Agricultural Show was held in the town and it was staged in Bridge Street in the field backing up to the New River Ancholme embankment. This carte-de-visite was produced by Thomas Smith of 47 Wrawby Street whose trade was cabinet making and upholstery. It shows the temporary arch erected on the bridge over the Ancholme to celebrate the show.

The workforce of Allen's Carriage Building works is gathered in front of the premises in Bridge Street displaying some examples of their craft. Engine Street can just be seen to the rear of the building. John Allen would have been keen to advertise the business he had taken over from Charles Marrows &s Son in around 1888 for he had come from Long Acre, London, with excellent credentials. When motor transport took over from horse-drawn vehicles, he went on to make bodies for cars and vans which were put onto Model T Ford chassis.

Bridge Street in Summer 1889. A lovely day when a glorious reception was given to Gervase Elwes, son of the Lord of the Manor and his bride Lady Winefride on their arrival in Brigg following their wedding 11 May 1889. The streets were lined with high Venetian masts, all the shops were closed and every house hung with flags. The newly-weds toured the town in a brake with four horses, beautiful bays, and two postilions.

This is clearly a market day as crowds throng the Market Place in front of the Angel Hotel. A typical Thursday, always well attended. Work commenced in 1896 to completely rebuild the frontage after it had weathered the elements for almost four hundred years. The result of this, together with other alterations and improvements, sees this still fine building dominating the scene today.

The firm of Spring & Co. expanded in the final decade of the nineteenth century, from small beginnings in Coney Court to large extensive works on the banks of the River Ancholme, close to the County Bridge. It soon acquired world-wide fame for its specialities of lemon curd and horseradish sauce, but is best remembered for jam making. Posing for the cameraman is a group from the workforce which grew larger and larger in the twentieth century.

An almost rural setting outside 36 Wrawby Street shown on a cabinet photograph taken by Alf Clark also of Wrawby Street. It shows a quiet children's group posing outside the building that was to become today's familiar public house, the Britannia. Reuben Blissett was a beer retailer here one hundred years ago when the building looked more like a private house. A similar doorway to this survives today in the house next door.

THE QUEEN'S DIAMOND JUBILEE,

JUNE 22nd, 1897

BRIGG OFFICIAL PROGRAMME

FOR THE DAY, INCLUDING

ORDER OF PROCESSION.

10 a.m.	Procession of Decorated Boats round the Island, headed by the Ancholme Rowing Club, and followed by the Steam Gondola "Stanley" with BAND, Council, and Committee on board. Seats may be booked by the public at a small charge. ☞ Other river craft invited.

IN THE MARKET PLACE.

11.	The full Complement of the **Wrawby Prize Brass Band** will play.
11-30.	The **Volunteers** will parade and fire a *Feu-de-Joie*.
11-35.	The **Public Bodies, Cyclists, School & other Children** will assemble for procession. ☞ The School Children over the age of 5, to meet at their respective Schools not later than 11 a.m.
11-45.	The **Address** to Her Majesty will be read from the "Angel" Balcony, and congratulatory telegram sent to the Queen.
12.	The **National Anthem**, conducted by Mr. C. W. Cray, will be sung. After which the Volunteers will fire another *Feu-de-Joie*.

THE PROCESSION

HAVING BEEN FORMED IN THE FOLLOWING ORDER :

The Band ;   The Volunteers ;   The Clergy and Ministers of the Town ;   The Chairman and Members of the Brigg Urban District Council ;   The Jubilee Chairmen with their several Committees ;   The Members of the Philanthropic Lodge of the Manchester Unity of the Independent Order of Oddfellows with their banners, &c. ;   The Members of the United Ancient Order of Druids with their banners, &c.;   The Fire Brigade, with their Engine ;   Other Public Bodies ;   The Cyclists with their Machines decorated or otherwise ;   The several School Children under their respective banners

Will march via Bridge Street, West Terrace, Forester Street, Wrawby Street, and Bigby Street, to the Elwes Street entrance to the Manor House Field.

IN THE MANOR HOUSE FIELD.

1 P.M.	**Dinner** to the Old People and Widows.
2.	**Sports** will commence.
3-30.	**Tea** to the Children will begin.
5-30.	Continuation and Completion of Sports.
7.	**Dancing** on the Green (the old Cricket pitch.)
9.	**Illuminated Procession of Cyclists**, from the Market Place round the Town to the Field.
9-15.	**Ascent of Fire Balloons**, with Magnesium lights.
9-30.	**Brilliant Illumination** of Coloured Fires.
9-45.	**Grand Ascent of Rockets**, with bright and brilliant and coloured stars.
10 p.m.	**BONFIRE** will be fired, to the accompaniment of

GOD SAVE THE QUEEN.

The Committee, acknowledging the kindness of the Lord of the Manor, in allowing them the use of the Manor House Field, earnestly ask the Public to assist them in carrying out the various items in an orderly manner, and particularly desire the Boys to abstain from any interference with the Bonfire.

Signed on behalf of the Decoration Committee,

S. P. HOLORAN,

This broadsheet was printed in 1897 to explain how Queen Victoria's Diamond Jubilee was to be celebrated in the town. There were many such special occasions during the Queen's long reign.

The town's inhabitants are gathered in the Market Place, 10 June 1897, for Queen Victoria's Diamond Jubilee festivities. The Brigg Volunteers, commanded by Lieut. Dove, are preparing to fire a *feu de joie*. Later a speech was made by Mr Sowter, Clerk to the Council, given from the balcony of the recently renovated Angel Hotel, and a procession was formed, led by the Wrawby Brass Band. A tour of the town ended at the Manor House Field where entertainment continued until 10 p.m.

This is Cary Lane. Although a lane, it is Brigg's bus station and is now so different. Just visible, centre, is the new Angel Hotel frontage of 1897. The nine white-washed cottages are long gone, as is the one to the left. The lane appeared to attract long-staying residents, rather than trades folk. The dominant building here is 9 Market Place, the offices of the Tadcaster Tower Brewery, now Barclays Bank.

Change Alley was one of the dark, narrow lanes off Wrawby Street, which was densely populated during the nineteenth century, but of which there is no trace today. The two posters announce the death of Queen Victoria, one covering the funeral details and the other telling of the local memorial service to be held at the Wesleyan Chapel. The Victorian era had ended.

Two

A New Century

This rare back-street view is of Elwes Street, taken from across the River Ancholme shows the point where it meets Cadney Road, *c.* 1902. Such a difference to what we see today, not a single building here remains. An interesting feature is the water tower soaring thirty-five feet into the sky, remembered only by Brigg's more senior residents. It was erected in about 1852 when the Elwes family piped in water to the eastern part of the town.

Brigg boasts few old buildings of architectural prominence, but the 'Old House' in Bigby Street, seen to the right of the card, is one. In the early 1900s it was also called the Old House School, catered mainly for girls and was privately run. Across the road two people are standing by a poster announcing another Cary Elwes organised concert. This family owned most of the town and lived in the large house just beyond the poster.

Stringer's Commercial and Temperance Hotel in around 1905. In this postcard view Richard Edward Stringer is offering cycle accommodation on both boards. It remained a hotel until the mid 1930s when it was transformed into Brigg's main post office. Seen here adjoining the building at 25 Bigby Street is the home of Dr Francis Goodman.

The Quaker movement was responsible for erecting this Friends Meeting House at the corner of Garden Street and Queen Street in 1863. With the decline of Quakerism in the town, it became the headquarters of the Liberal Association until the 1920s. Local activists have very little to smile about following the defeat of their candidate, the Hon. Frederick Guest by Sir Berkeley Sheffield in the 1907 by-election. Demolition took place in around 1960.

Wrawby Street with no traffic to worry a dog sitting at the crossroads where the war memorial was to be erected a generation later. Smoke pouring from the chimney indicates there is activity at Sutton Bean's Brewery, making a good pint to be enjoyed at the Britannia Inn or the Queen's Arms situated to either side of it!

Walter E. Cottew's shop at 5 Wrawby Street. Most importantly to us, this stationer, bookseller and newsagent sold and printed early postcard views of the town. By 1905 Arthur Megson had taken over the business and by 1907 Walter Bee Robinson superseded him. He stayed until after the Second World War, but prior to 1914 he produced some excellent, real photographic postcards of Brigg and district. Some of them were used in this book.

It is hard to believe initially that this is a Brigg view, but these new dwellings were classed as 'New Brigg'. Mr Dent, foreman builder, with his family, is proudly standing outside 72 Grammar School Road.

Turning through 180 degrees the photographer here shows the other 'new, neat and convenient' residences of Grammar School Road. The residents were promised 'reasonable rents' and with 'better roads' it would soon become 'Brigg's most eligible suburb'. These children are standing outside Nos 52 and 50 Westmoor Villas.

Wrawby Street, 1909. A real collector's card: real photographic material with 'animation' and plenty of interest. The Union of London and Smiths Bank dwarfs the tailor's shop of Mrs Anne Eaton next door at No. 9. Amongst the shoppers and on-lookers beyond Sarah White's Dining Rooms at No. 67 can be spied Mrs Isabella Otter's bakery cart outside No. 62. James Jackson at No. 66, and Charles Stubbs at No. 68, both grocers vying for the same customers.

Thomas Jackson started his grocery business at 66 Wrawby Street in the early 1880s, with a bakery at the rear. By about 1907, young James Jackson had taken over the shop. He can be seen here in the doorway with hams hanging above him. Little Edith Jackson, his daughter, is by his side. Charles Davies is the other shop worker, whilst young H. Snell is posing with the firm's handcart; he later became a church minister.

'We are having grand weather', writes the sender of this superb view 13 August 1909. Here is Edwardian Brigg and it appears idyllic. The ladies are showing off the latest fashions and look very attractive as they pass by G.W. Green's drapery just beyond the Lord Nelson Hotel. Green's store offered millinery at exceptional prices including smart London copies, and dressmaking style and fit was guaranteed.

This real photographic postcard of the Market Place was posted in 1911. It shows a typical Lincolnshire Thursday market where motorised transport is not yet apparent, although the garage is advertising motorcars for hire, above the archway. Here also is the long gone Ancholme Inn on the brow of the County Bridge over the River Ancholme, advertised as 'the noted fishing club of Brigg'. It had been acquired and updated by Ind Coope at the end of the century.

Allen's the confectioners in the Market Place. Every shop provided a delivery service, which meant a job for a young lad, and Allen's was no exception. Their little cart can be seen parked in front of the business William Allen established in 1874. It included a restaurant and continued for over thirty-five years until it was taken over by Walter Chafen in around 1910.

Brigg gasworks, 1910. The men by the retort are casual workers except Harry Hardy, in collar and tie, the manager of The Ancholme Packet Company on the river's edge next to these works. Jim Holland, standing in the centre on the front row, is the town's gaslighter. It was his job at dusk to walk around the town putting on all the street lights and at midnight going around extinguishing them.

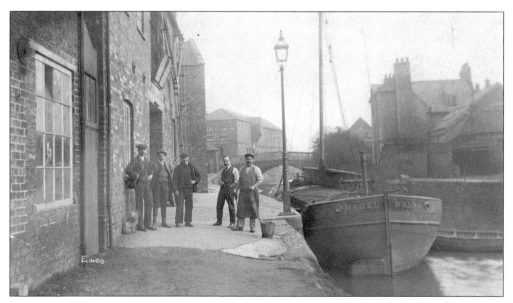

The barge *Mabel* is tied up outside the Ancholme Packet Company on the River Ancholme in 1912. The manager, Harry Hardy, is standing second from the right. In the centre of the group is barge skipper, Albert Neall, who usually sailed on *Togi*. He knew the journey to and from Hull like the back of his hand. Close to the skipper is local boatman and fisherman, Jim Holland, waiting to do some loading and unloading of cargoes.

Gervase and Lady Winefrede Elwes started the Brigg Musical Festival at the turn of the twentieth century and by 1905 it had become a flourishing institution. At the Children's Festivals held in the grounds of the Manor House, children are seen performing on the lawn, accompanied by Gervase Elwes, watched by the grown-ups and making a very pretty picture.

Written on the front of this 1906 postcard are the words 'Making New Rifle Range, Manley Gardens Brigg'. This is a bit of a mystery as the only rifle club known in the town over the years was in Foundry Lane, but perhaps that was close enough for the postcard writer!

Special occasions always bring out the crowds and in Brigg they also used to bring out the photographers, Wilmore and Sons, of Bridge Street. This spectacle is in West Terrance, 11 July 1908, when the local solicitor, Frank C. Hett, Esq. laid a foundation stone for the new Salvation Army Hall. Notice the photographer with his tripod on the upper left of the picture. Notice also the eyes of the crowd.

This is a continuation of the events in the above postcard view. It is most unusual to see Edwardian photographers at work, but here one is seen snapping the other. Probably very few Brigg folk would recognise this back street picture showing the corner, with a gas-lamp, of Engine Street and West Terrace. Beyond the busy photographer are the roofs of Happyland, which was a small hidden area of housing, off Bridge Street..

General Election 1910. A crowd has gathered within the precincts of the Corn Exchange, 22 January 1910, to hear the result of the General Election announced by the returning officer, Mr Scorer. Photographers took up their stands about midday with cameras focussed to take snapshots when the Corn Exchange doors were opened, and the declaration was made. Sir Alfred Gelder, Liberal, defeated Sir Berkeley Sheffield, Tory, by 237 votes.

After the declaration, the crowd made its way to the Market Place, and the victor was escorted by a posse of policemen to Mr Elwood's shop. In this photograph the Liberal supporters are seen surging around the establishment to hear Sir Alfred's address, accompanied by Lady Gelder and other party workers.

The Proclamation of George V on 17 May 1910 – at one o'clock. The scene is outside Brigg's old police station as Mr J. Cliff of Scawby Grove reads out the proclamation with much expression. The thoroughfare is completely blocked as the time for performing the ceremony arrives.

The proclamation ceremony was later performed in the Market Place, and again in Bridge Street outside the Brocklesby Ox Inn opposite the old Recreation Ground. A procession was formed to tour the town from one ceremony to another led by Supt. Reed on horseback, the police, the band, Territorials, magistrates, the vicar of Brigg and others. Here the procession is passing through Queen Street.

A fire at the Yarborough Oil Mills broke out on Sunday morning 22 May 1910. Help was needed from the Grimsby Fire Brigade to fight one of the most disastrous fires in the history of Brigg. Members of the brigade are pictured at the scene, on the bank of the River Ancholme.

Despite copious amounts of water being poured onto the building, the mill fire spread. The quantity of debris which was deposited in the river, reached several feet above the surface of the water and with a strong breeze blowing the flames gained the upper hand. The huge structure eventually surrendered.

Brigg Grammar School, c. 1910. In January 1910, Mr H.E. Bryant BA was appointed headmaster and success was to follow after a temporary closure in 1906. The boys here appear well kitted out, complete with school caps, as they pose during PT for the cameraman, perhaps for the preparation of a new school prospectus! This is a very formally posed picture taken in the school quadrangle, with bicycle shed and old 'chemi' lab in the background.

Wilmore, the Brigg photographer, clearly didn't have the fast shutter speeds available today for his action shots. Even in the school sports, it appears that the boy doing the high jump still hangs on to the school cap with the 'Fortitudine' motto on the badge. School uniforms were very important.

On a hot summer's day, 22 June 1911, the coronation of George V was celebrated with a varied programme of events. In the afternoon the decorated rullies containing happy children from the various Sunday schools paraded around the town. Grayson Clarke, newly from Scotter and living in Gelder Terrance, caught the procession with his camera in Bridge Street on the way to the county show field for judging.

The Congregational church was awarded first prize for the best decorated rully. The children were Winnie Young, representing England; Dorothy Kershaw, Scotland; Rebecca Dent, Ireland; Sarah Bullivant, Wales; W. Leeson, the King; R. Kettle, the King's page and Miss Roberts, the Maid of Honour. In the background are seen the sheds in course of erection for the Lincolnshire Show which was to be held in three weeks time.

Jackson's the printers was long established in the Market Place and stocked pianos, gramophones, organs and sheet music. In their window is the official Coronation programme for all to read. The local photographer of this postcard is Wilmore, who already in the press, is advertising his animated films of the festivities to be shown the following week at the town hall.

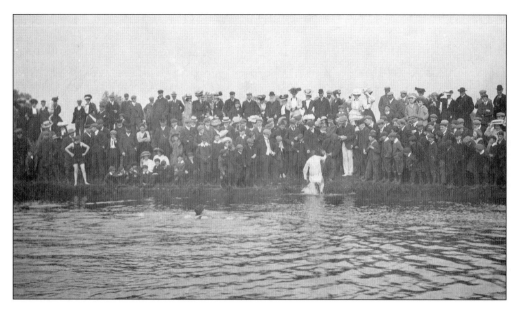

Celebrations for the Coronation of George V in 1911. What do we make of this? It is apparently a 'top hat and shirt race' in the river carnival sports. C.W. Davies, the winner, in his wet shirt is being helped out, whilst W. Jenkins in midstream, but still wearing his top hat, has a little way to go. Oh happy days!

Such a very long line of omnibuses was the sight greeting the people of Brigg on Thursday, 12 July 1911 for the County Show. These buses stretched the whole length of Bridge Street. For three days the Lincolnshire Agricultural Society held its forty-first exhibition here. The function took place at Brigg once every decade and the town rose to the occasion with elaborate displays of bunting and flags.

The venue for the County Show in 1911 was the field abutting the New River Ancholme on Bridge Street. The fields were admirably enclosed and all kinds of wooden structures were erected to meet the requirements of both exhibitors and visitors alike. A principal feature of the show was the tradesmen's stands.

To postcard collectors unravelling a mystery postcard picture successfully is truly exciting. This card bearing a message written in shorthand was postmarked Brigg 1911, and apparently shows General Baden Powell. Did the hero of Mafeking come to Brigg? Apparently he did, for one Monday night, 22 May 1911, to inspect his local troops in the Corn Exchange.

Bradley's shop at 14 Wrawby Street. Anthony Bradley opened his clothiers shop in about 1904, and the firm became a feature of Brigg for the next sixty years or more. It specialised in ready-to-wear clothing for boys, youths and men, especially the working man. In School Court can be seen beer barrels for the Butchers Arms and beyond the man is a sign offering 'Good Beds for Travellers'.

The Engine House in 1916. A letter from a lady in Canada, researching her family tree, resulted in us unearthing this wonderful old picture. Many generations of the Thompson family, pictured here, were in charge of the pumping station on the bank of the River Ancholme towards Cadney. They lived in the house adjacent to it which is still standing today but is unoccupied and almost derelict.

In 1885 the firm of aerated water manufacturers, J.W. White & Sons, were in Coney Court, but by 1892 it had moved here in Elwes Street opposite Paradise Place. Locally known as the 'Popworks', it was a feature until the late 1960s.

Wrawby Street, c. 1913. Today's generation will find the names of all the shops illustrated here unfamiliar, yet for decades they did not change. Hunters Tea Stores, Eccles the tailor, and Dunn's footwear will be recognised by the over-forties. The little girls catch one's eye – such pretty hats and dresses are a far cry from today.

The Brigg Victorias were reckoned a 'plum' team as winners of the Scunthorpe Junior A.F. Tournament, Saturday 25 April 1914, just before the war. One wonders how many survived as young soldiers. The team was as follows: A. White (captain), H. Tingay (vice-captain), R.H. Westoby, A. Draper, E. Leeson, L. Hayman, J. Neal (hon. sec.), E. Parkinson, E.F. Brown, J. Thorpe, B. Harrison. J. Leaning (first reserve), F. Hotson (trainer).

War Comes to Brigg. Following a service at St John's church, conducted by Canon Claye, on Thursday 6 August 1914, the first batch of Brigg Territorials prepare to leave for active service. There are many serious faces as the two officers, Lieut. G. Sowter and Sgt. R.G. Glover, centre left, organise the young men for the march to the station to board the 9.38 a.m. train. Their immediate destination was Grimsby.

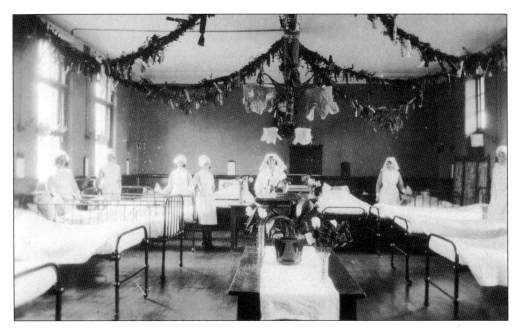

The new infirmary at the workhouse was described by Revd Godfrey as 'a building, bright internally, providing the best treatment in most comfortable surroundings' after he had performed the opening ceremony on Thursday, 18 November 1915. Dr Goodman, medical officer at the workhouse for thirty-four years, enthused over such an up-to-date institution. A month later, amid Christmas spirit, the nursing staff posed for this photograph in their new ward.

The war nears its conclusion and an era ends. These two ladies, with their children, pass the time of day at the corner of West Terrace and Bridge Street. Stretching from the entrance to Happyland, these white painted cottages, (Nos 18–21) and Nos 1 and 2 West Terrace survived until bought and demolished in 1938. West Terrace (Nos. 3–9) were lived in until the 1960s, but only No. 3 remains today.

Cadney Road in around 1919. The river and road run into Brigg together. The lime trees, planted at past Victorian celebrations, have flourished, but the names of some previous local shopkeepers have faded with time on the wall at the end of the towpath.

Three
Between the Wars

Peace Celebrations in 1919. Brigg's festivities spread over two days, Friday 18 July and Saturday 19 July. Saturday was 'Everybody's Day', whereas Friday was for the children. The parade around the town had many praiseworthy designs. Here one group of decorated cycles is seen passing the old police station and heading towards the new war memorial.

MONUMENT ERECTED TO THE MEMORY
OF NOT FALLEN BRIGG HEROES.

A moving scene at the war memorial which bore further emblems of respect to those who had died. The postcard writer explains, 'Mrs Whiteley is in the trap as a Red Cross nurse'.

A small group of children gather at the war memorial, Sunday 15 June 1919, after the crowds have gone. In the centre is Francis Ashton and on the extreme left is Gladys Scuffham. Earlier the monument had been unveiled by Mrs Stamp on behalf of her husband, Cllr Harry Stamp JP, the generous donor. Coincidentally the same day Alcock and Brown, the aviators, landed in Co. Galway after a 16-hour flight over the Atlantic from Newfoundland.

In December 1919 the Elwes family sold off a large part of their estate in and around Brigg. The White Horse in Wrawby Street was described at auction as having a bar, smoke room, tap room and sitting room, all with fireplaces, plus a back kitchen, dairy and scullery. Upstairs were four bedrooms, boxroom and sitting room. Outside were a valuable paddock, stabling and a pair of cottages. It was bought by Mr Bean.

Tollbar Farm on Bigby High Road was also sold by the Elwes family. It consisted of 103 acres and was advertised as having a drawing room, dining room, kitchen with sink, and dairy. Upstairs were three bedrooms, and outside a coalhouse and closet.

Anyone for hockey? The Girls' High School team for 1921/22 comprised, from left to right, standing: -?-, G. Sumpter, Violet Sumpter, Gwendoline Dent, Mabel Dickinson. Kneeling: Lucy Smith, Molly Young, -?- , Mary Herring, Dora Lusby. Seated: Dorothy Frankland.

The Bloodworth family ready for Thursday market with a magnificent display of cauliflowers on their cart and providing a photographic opportunity for Grayson Clarke. The location is Mill Lane close to Bell's Mill where successive generations of the Bloodworth family were in business as market gardeners.

At John Thompson's haircutting and shaving saloon, situated on the corner of Bridge Street and Forester Street, you could also get your umbrella repaired. The price for a complete recovering started at 2/6d, with special prices given for larger umbrellas. John was tragically drowned whilst swimming in the River Ancholme close to his parent's home at the Engine House in July 1921.

The greengrocer's shop on the corner of Bridge Street and Kiln Lane belonged in the mid-1920s to Charles and Annie Bloodworth. His brother ran the market gardening venture in Mill Lane close by. The couple continued their business until his death in around 1953. The houses of Alexandria Terrace (stone dated 1883) remain but the terraced homes of Kiln Lane are gone, although still inhabited into the 1960s.

The building and contracting firm of R.M. Phillips has its scaffolding erected on the former Manor House of the Elwes family who had left Brigg in 1913. They generously gave the building to the Rosminian Sisters in 1919 who opened the Manor House Convent School on 30 September 1921. The school closed at the end of the summer term 1971.

During the 1920s, new houses were built for the council by Messrs R.M. Phillips. They had been badly needed for many years, as the condition of housing in the town was generally very poor. Woodbine Avenue, the first stage to be developed is to the left side, with Central Square to the right.

BIGBY STREET, BRIGG.

Bigby Street in around 1925. The church tower rises above the other properties, where on the right is the ivy clad building of Hett's solicitors and the Hackfords' residence. Nearer to the church are the United Methodist chapel and the Church House, both gone by 1966. On the opposite side is the Manor House Convent and in the distance the large furnishing store belonging to Mr J.T. Kettle.

Bigby Street in around 1926. Miss Elsie Hackford opened a confectioners and tobacconist shop at No. 8 Bigby Street, by converting the front part of the property featured on the picture above. Miss Norah Clark took over the business in the mid-1930s and it became a popular tuck shop with the convent girls from across the street for the next twenty-five years.

A fading, rather anonymous postcard view of Woodbine Farm in the very early 1920s. The postal address was Wrawby Road and it was run by John Robert Willey. In the 1930s William Hill acquired the farm, but for many locals it has been Brigg's Recreation ground for the last fifty years. Until 1974, when it was demolished, this building was the groundsman's home and office.

Erected adjacent to No. 1 Woodbine Avenue in about 1925, this wooden structure was constructed by Frederic East, a master coachbuilder, for his wife Louisa. It was a general store and sub post office. Although the latter facility ceased before the war, the shop remained until the 1950s. Their son, Harry, is pictured outside the doorway in about 1929.

Sutton Bean's Brewery opened a retail shop in 1896 at 4 Queen Street for the convenience of its smaller customers. With the closure of the Brigg brewery in 1924, the shop was purchased, with other property by the Hull Brewery Co. Their first manager was Jack Beeston, followed by George East, who continued in charge for several decades until his retirement.

A Sunday School Union gathering. Over 400 happy youngsters would assemble for this century-old custom in the Market Place and clamber on to the variously decorated carts, like this group posing here before the procession. Later in the programme they would be taken to their respective schools for tea, followed by three hours of sports at Woodbine Farm, kindly lent for the occasion.

A quiet view in the 1920s looking towards Scawby and Hibaldstow station on the London and North Eastern Railway. A solitary porter's barrow is by the high chimneyed house of the stationmaster, George Saxby. At the distant end of the station are wagons in the sidings depositing coal at the local merchants' yards.

Underneath the tall maturing limes in Bigby Street 1929 is a captured German gun. It had been pulled round the town as part of the peace parade in 1919, then positioned here, where it remained until the Second World War. These buildings are private residences, although Arthur Jackson had his dental surgery at No. 16, and Drs Goodman and Holme were in practice at No. 25.

J.H. Jackson's shop at 66 Wrawby Street. Time moves on; it's now post-war with a new frontage. Jimmy Jackson has been in charge for, maybe, fifteen years, longer than the lives of young F. Rhodes and B. Cross. Mr Jackson looks content in the doorway, but both he and Charles Davies (to his left) have naturally aged from the pre-war photograph in this book. Mr Smith, hands on hips, is the baker.

In contrast to the grander shopfronts of the retailers close to the market area, those at the eastern end of Wrawby Street tended to be quite simple. Smaller shops often consisting of just the front room of a house and much less commercial looking were the norm. A typical example is this confectionery and tobacconist business belonging to Charles Leaning at 50 Wrawby Street in the 1920s.

The Market Place in around 1930. The thoroughfare has been recently tarmacked, but some cobbles remain causing complaints from pedestrians. The National Provincial Bank has just built its new premises, and since the war Barclays Bank has replaced the Tadcaster Tower Brewery offices. Next door, Melias, the grocers, has appeared where Anthony, the drapers, was before the war. Traffic is more notable, both with road signs and motors.

The huge building in the background provides the clue to the whereabouts of this game of tennis – it is the Corn Exchange. In addition to tennis courts, a bowling green could be found behind the Angel Hotel and Midland Bank. This was a time of peace and happiness – halcyon days!

The Royal Picture Playhouse in around 1930. Back in 1911 the Wilmore Brothers, photographers of Bridge Street, were advertising animated cinematograph films of the Brigg Coronation Festivities and Scawby Gull Ponds to be shown at the town hall. A year later they had moved to the larger Corn Exchange. At the end of the war, the Wilmores were listed as the proprietors of the Electric Picture Playhouse at this building. Mr G.H. Wilson had become the lessee and manager in the early 1920s but by 1930 he was facing stiff new competition 'where the sound sounds sweetest', – so read the posters!

The building of Brigg's first purpose built cinema, The Grand, was the idea of local businessmen. Here, on this card, these men appear to be waiting for the final touches to be applied to the nearly completed article in 1928. When it opened, it was in style. For a few years in the 1930s, the two cinemas competed one against the other, but there was only one winner – 'Brigg's Super Cinema'.

For just over sixty years, after full production first started in 1929, local residents came to recognise the sweet, rather sickly smell that drifted over the district during the Autumn and Winter. Here the beet campaign was in full swing at the Brigg sugar factory on the outskirts of the town. The smell is now gone, but sadly so have the jobs.

A lorry belonging to Martin and Watson, haulage contractors, is parked outside Slater's garage in Bridge Street in 1930 – now the Jet petrol station. The haulage firm started with steam wagons and was based at the Nelthorpe Arms yard nearby until the early 1930s, when it transferred to the Britannia Garage opposite the police station. These new premises had formerly been the Sutton Bean's brewery.

Bridge Street in around 1935. A lady rests at Fisher's shop, perhaps needing a cup of tea at May Hunter's, or something stronger at Bert Gilliatt's Brocklesby Ox pub. Over the street by Allen's rather run down coach building premises, is the shop of George Sowerby, the cobbler at the alleyway to Happyland. By 1939 the tenants of the white cottages had moved due to redevelopment.

Barge traffic was the lifeline to Brigg's trade and industry. Viewed here in about 1925 from the County Bridge, one barge is moored at Sergeant's Brewery wharf, whilst beyond, by the gasworks, in midstream, another is unloading coal, - a precarious job for the man on the plank. Spring's jam factory is to the right.

The County Bridge in 1934. The Ancholme gently flows under the stone arch here just as it does today. Since it was built in 1828 time and the elements have rendered it less attractive and secure. The traditional but eroded balustrades were replaced in 1962 by metal rails. The elegant gas lamps are long gone and so is the toll booth.

Spring's delights in 1932. Happy smiles from Spring's workers pictured on the riverbank, close to the old toll booth. Back row, left to right: Emily Flear, Olive Fisher, Mary Markham, Netta Neal, Maggie Jenkins, Ellen Sipling, Iris Bird, Ivy Dunderdale, Kathleen Button, Betty Fisher, Doris Holmes, Gladys East. Front row: Edna Leeson, Charlotte Thistleton, Phyllis Chapman, Annie Sipling, Alice Squires, Beatrice (Beatie) Neal, Rene Bird, Daisy Leedham.

The Delecta Cake Shop in the late 1930s. This confectioner's shop was run by Miss Victoria Smith, who according to the sign above the doorway was also licensed to sell tobacco. The shop was at No. 65 Wrawby Street, next to Jimmy Jackson's grocery. The young lady in the doorway is Miss Dorothy Machin who married George Watson, the Worlaby blacksmith.

When Lacey and Clark refurbished their premises in 1927, the Corner House Café was opened upstairs serving morning coffee, afternoon tea and light refreshments. 'The highest quality food with excellent service in a bright atmosphere' was how it was advertised – 'The perfect rendezvous'.

An Urban District Council road gang are taking a rest from repairing Brigg's roads close to the Monument in the 1930s. 'Prim' Watkin, second from the left is the well established foreman. We can see the basic tools for the men - tar barrel, boiler, barrows and shovel as they pose in front of houses that were much later converted into Sass's car showrooms.

Wrawby Road in 1935. The road into Brigg from Wrawby, with its avenue of lime trees, is as picturesque as anywhere in the country. The view can still be enjoyed today, although the buildings in the distance have changed. You can no longer buy a car from Mr Sass or sweets from Samuel Chamberlain's shop, neither can you fill up your motor car from Bryant Brothers' BP petrol pump.

Opposite: Bigby Street in 1935 with a full-length view of St John's church. George Badley, the jeweller, has recently moved in at No. 4. Next door is Miss Mary Lyne's needlework and knitting shop and nearby is Norah Clark's confectionery (No. 8) with her teashop at the side. The long established Exchange Club is ahead.

Grammar School Road. In the last decade, this road has now been cut across by Brigg's busy internal bypass, the only building casualties being the pair of houses by the dog in this photograph. The electricity services van is parked close to Chapman & Son, the blacksmiths and schoolboys can be seen leaving the grammar school.

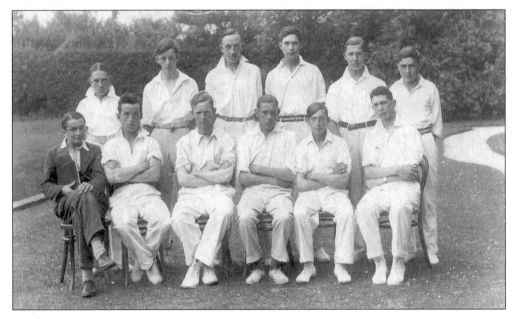

The Grammar School cricket team. Most Briggensian families have photographs to remember their schooldays by. Here is the school team of 1930. Back row, left to right: P.F. Brown, J. Ure, R.A. Binns, J.T. Thompson, J.W. Osgerby, F. Marris. Front row: R.A. Walker, W.M. Thomas, H.E. Howson, D.A. Denton, G. Kitching, R.W. Parton.

This picture was used in the 1935 Brigg Grammar School prospectus. However, this open air swimming bath had been in regular summer use since 1915 and for the next forty-two years it was where we grammer schoolboys learned to swim – unless we used the River Ancholme.

The family firm of grocers, Joseph Burton & Sons, splashed out to proclaim the coronation of King George VI and Queen Elizabeth on 12 May 1937. No. 58 Wrawby Street was aflame with bunting of red, white and blue, and photographs of the royal couple hung over the doorway and on the door.

Coronation Day, 12 May 1937. A rainy day that could have dampened Brigg's festive spirit, but by 9.15 a.m. the procession was assembled in the Market Place. Brigg Prize Silver Band, led by veteran bass player Tom Leeson, headed the parade en route to the Grammar School quadrangle for a united thanksgiving service.

It's the late 1930s but Brigg's views remain tranquil. Two mothers with their offspring chat outside Belle Vue Villas next to Chamberlain's shop. Just one vehicle is visible at what is now a busy junction. Two strange lamps seem to have been fixed at the monument – is it preparation for what is to come?

64

Four

The Second World War and Beyond

War was declared in 1939 so the Union Jack is to the fore and the annual crowning of the May Queen at Glebe Road School goes on as it has done since 1932. Miss Strickland, a teacher, probably took the photographs. Dorothy Denton was the Queen in 1940 when this was taken. Left to right: Helen Thacker, Sylvia Steeper, Doreen Firmedow, Nancy Leeson, Dorothy Denton, Dulcie Skinner, Nellie Boston, -?-, -?-, -?-, Margaret Collins. Those in front are evacuees.

Glebe Road school staff. Between 1940-45 school life was hectic with interruptions for air raid warnings, holidays for potato picking and salvage collections. The staff changed too but to many these faces will be familiar. Back row, left to right: Miss Clark, Mr Armstrong, Miss Stringer, Mr Booth, Mrs Bratley, -?- . Front row: Miss Craig, Miss Nichols, Mr Bratley (head), Mrs Silverwood, Miss Marrows.

BRIGG GRAMMAR SCHOOL.

AUTUMN TERM 1943.

The Autumn Term will commence on Tuesday, 31st August and end on Tuesday, 21st December. There will be a break from 1st October to 1st November so that members of the School may help in the lifting of potatoes and sugar beet.

I regret this interruption with the normal work of the School, but the increased demand for assistance on the farm calls us to offer all the help possible. During the last three years masters and boys of the School have rendered great service in helping to harvest valuable food stuffs.

J. T. DAUGHTON.

The head's letter to the parents would have seemed quite mundane to the schoolboys for war must have dominated their lives. They recall watching the blitz on Hull, of scouts riding round as messengers, of dashing to the shelter at night. They remember the head in his ARP warden's hat and the counting of bombers leaving the surrounding 'dromes.

This card of the Market Place was posted in 1944 but there's no sign of war here. Ford cars are outside E.H. Smith's garage and across the way is Hepworth & Son, clothiers, and next door at No. 28 is Taylor's Drug Co.

The Rabbit Club held a special show in August each year when, in addition to trophies, the winners also received prizes supplied by Badleys jewellers. The 1944 committee is pictured in the yard behind the home of Mr and Mrs Empson on Bigby Road where the meetings were held. Standing, left to right: George Winterbottom, Herbert Wilcox, John Chapman, Arthur Lavington, Wilf Green, Ron Hilton. Seated: Bill Empson, Dora Empson, Elsie Stringer, Stan Bones.

VE celebrations, June 1945. Brigg was awash with children's VE parties throughout June and July, stretching into August, with VJ parties to follow. The fancy dress entrants on Fergus Proctor's lorry in this procession are being looked after by Councillor George Hewson. Amongst this group of excited youngsters are Barbara Roberts, Betty Bird, Mary White and Ann Chafen.

The Bridge Street victory procession in 1945 leaves the Market Place escorted by Sergeant Atton and Ernie Taylor's faithful loudspeaker system. A smiling Mabel Goodhand from Engine Street adjusts her headscarf as she walks with her friend Pearl Mason towards the Brocklesby Ox field to join in the tea party and fun.

THE ANNUAL GENERAL MEETING of the Club will be held at the Black Bull Hotel, on Monday, April 30th, 1945, at 7·30 p.m., to confirm the Hon. Treasurer's accounts for the year ending 31st March, 1945, to elect Officers for the coming year, and to deal with any other business.

Your attendance is particularly requested.

Westrum Lane,   F. HENTHORN,
   Brigg,   Hon. Secretary.
16th April, 1945.

Ancholme Rowing Club continued throughout the war years. Although men left to join the forces, other visiting servicemen joined the club. Women also joined due to male shortage with Ruth Briggs being captain in 1943. Dr Frank Henthorn joined the club in May 1933 and remained a member all his long life, eventually writing *The History of Brigg Rowing Club*.

Ancholme Rowing Club on a Sunday morning on the river by Cadney Road. It has not changed much from this photograph of two single sculls, rated more as training craft, taken after the end of the war. Today the club boasts a membership of eighty or more and remains active on the regatta circuit.

Brigg Silver Band in 1949. Bandmaster Laurie Mumby prepares members for a blow at the new bandroom in Chapel Yard off Wrawby Street. Back row, left to right: John Robinson, Jack Robinson, Vin East, Alf Rands, George Foster. Middle row: John Horstead, Billy Leeson, Colin Miller, David Rands, Fred West, Brian Blakey. Front row: Andrew Tedder, John Saberton, Ted Saberton, Harry East.

Wrawby Street, c. 1950. A quiet market town setting with the community doing its daily shopping. There is just the odd cycle parked outside Hunter's Tea Store and a car outside the gardeners' shop of Pennells. Across the street between the pubs and shops are narrow alley-ways and yards, now all gradually disappearing. In the far distance is the smoking chimney of Brigg's Workhouse.

The Brocklesby Ox in 1946 and the bus is parked in the pub yard ready to take the back room customers on their annual outing to Skegness. Landlady, Nellie Clark, makes sure there is plenty of liquid refreshment for the day. Loading the barrels on to the bus are Ted Brown, Charlie Taylor, Joe Fowler and Jack Boston, while Harold Taylor looks on.

Bridge Street, c. 1950. A horse and cart holds up the traffic but this card is dominated by the number of buses, at a time when cars were still few. The Market Rasen bus awaits its passengers outside Dr King's surgery next to the little sweet and tobacconist shop of Miss White.

The Glanford Players performing *The Carpet Slipper* at the Corn Exchange, *c.* 1951. Standing, left to right: Jean Proctor, -?-, Mary Pimlott, Raymond Barker, Grace Van Den Bos, Marjorie Thompson, Mary Barker, Alice Dickinson. Seated: Vic Parker. If you wore the magic slippers you were whisked off to strange exotic places – that was the idea. Once a year in October, on a Thursday, Friday and Saturday, the society performed a well-received play which was produced, for many years, by Ruth Briggs.

Market Day, *c.* 1950. Traffic could pass safely both ways through the Market Place at this time, with perhaps one policemen standing directing traffic where the two streets fork at Edlington's farm implements 'hut'. The Angel Hotel was *the* meeting place for the local farmers and the traders and shoppers enjoyed Massarella's ice creams.

Station Road, *c.* 1950. The government of the day embarked on a policy of nationalisation which included the road haulage industry. All the lorries, belonging to local hauliers were commandeered under the scheme, and parked en masse in Station Road during the reorganisation. Their garages were taken over too and everything was to be under one name – British Road Services.

During 1953 the old workhouse buildings were modernised by the installation of new windows and central heating and it was renamed 'Crosslands'. It ceased to function as a workhouse under the National Assistance Act 1948 and became a home mainly for the elderly. It consisted of three blocks; the men are standing in front of the rear block and the infirmary is just visible to the right.

Spring's Delights were established in 1875 as makers of preserves and were large employers of Brigg women. At this time Spring's products were distributed throughout the whole of Britain and the export trade, enjoyed before the war, was steadily rebuilt. Each year the firm went to London, with some chosen workers, to promote their goods at the Olympia Show. It lasted several days.

This arch over the River Ancholme was a highlight of the town's decorations for the coronation of Queen Elizabeth on 2 June 1953. It was supplied and paid for by Spring's Delights whose talented joiner, Ted Lamming, was mainly responsible for its impressive construction. On Coronation Day itself, almost continuous rain and high winds spoiled Brigg's plans for a parade, children's sports and a six-a-side football match.

The Angel Hotel, seen here in about 1953, dominated the Market Place and to youngsters like us the interior, on entering through the revolving doors, was a different world. Vines hung from the glass-covered courtyard with its Lloyd Loom style furniture and by the office entrance was the door to the 'men only' room. Beyond that was the lounge where a maid awaited.

Ladies Football Team, c. 1948. A little of the post-war depression must surely have been lifted by a charity match played on the Brocklesby Ox ground. The opposition was a team of men dressed as ladies. From left to right, back row: Nora Yates, Marion Spight, Stella Pigott, Winnie Altoft, ? Standerline. Front row: Marcella Bingley, Dorry Yates, Ann Standerline, Mary Standerline, Nellie Clark, Miriam Taylor.

Brigg Town Reserves photographed on the Brocklesby Ox ground with another trophy, c. 1950. They are, back row, left to right: Charlie Petch, -?-, Ted Boston (trainer), Jack Durrant, Johnny Bingley, -?-, Clem Trafford, Joe Fowler, Ray Fisher, Tom Daubney. Middle row: Basil Neall, Jim Holland, Don Denton, -?-. Front row: Ted Haith. Len Fisher, Tom Fowler, -?-, Ron Broome.

The Horse Fair, 5 August 1955. The tradition of horse traders invading the town for two or three days to try to sell their animals was a colourful annual event. The business involved hectic activity as the horses, young and old, were put through their paces in front of possible buyers, on Brigg's main streets. The calm and orderly scene here outside the Grand cinema and Horse Fair Paddock in Wrawby Street was apparently not always so!

Five
Vanishing Brigg

Looking over this parapet of the County Bridge in the 1960s locals would have thought that Brigg and Spring's Jams were synonymous and that the firm would always be found nestling here in the heart of the town on the bank of the River Ancholme. It grew from humble beginnings in the 1870s to a respected, nationally known company and Brigg's largest employer. Assurances were given in the early 1970s following financial difficulties, but in early 1980 the factory closed. We hope this picture and some of the following ones will be a reminder of some familiar sights only recently lost.

Bridge Street in the 1970s. This side of the street had become rather run down and was ready for redevelopment. Here some families still live and some little shops have closed forever while others are just open temporarily. This was a part of Bridge Street that really thrived in past generations, but is now all gone. These properties, along with some in Grammar School Road, were demolished when work started on Brigg's bypass in June 1991.

E.H. Smith ironmongers, c. 1978. Few firms had such a record of service behind them as this one, which carried on the same business, on the same site, for nearly 350 years, beginning in 1625. The shop closed in the summer of 1966 and a few years later, after sustaining damage when hit by a lorry, the shop and building had to come down. No. 2 Market Place was no more.

The Grand cinema has now gone and a very busy internal bypass runs precisely where the building stood. To local youngsters during its prime this was the only place to be on Saturday afternoons of the 1940s and 1950s. It closed in 1965 and this is a sad picture of it in the 1970s sitting empty and unwanted.

Brigg railway station. Unfortunately many small stations have disappeared as car ownership has removed much of the need but at least Brigg still has a station, just a stopping point now. Even in the 1970s, when this photograph was taken, it looked imposing, but there are no buildings there now, no stationmaster's house and no waiting rooms.

Draper Bros, decorators, of Wrawby Street in 1971. The closed sign had gone up on the shop door and, together with the other two shops, was soon to become a memory. Radical redevelopment of the site is soon to take place. Change Alley and Garden Alley, uninhabited for decades, will disappear without a trace. The Donkey Derby poster in the window is for June 1971.

Wrawby Street in 1982 with modern shop units replacing the old buildings. In September 1975 Pailthorp, the jewellers, arrived bringing joy for the ladies if not for the men, and they have survived! The nationwide firms of Baxters and Radio Rentals were very short-lived. By late 1982 Brigg Photolabs had replaced Radio Rentals and Oxfam later became Brigg's first charity shop.

Probably the largest building in Wrawby Street, this was once the home of Ralph Musgrave, the furrier, and it became a bank in 1861. The folk of Brigg knew it as 'Woollies' from its opening just before the war until its closure in 1983 when the 'Wonder of Woollies' had lost its sparkle and another familiar name was lost from the town.

Monument Works garage was still advertising cars in the local press in the early 1980s, but by 1983 closing down signs were evident in the windows. William Sass had started his motor engineering business here in 1924 and the premises had expanded over the decades. Unfortunately, in the same era, other Brigg garages folded too.

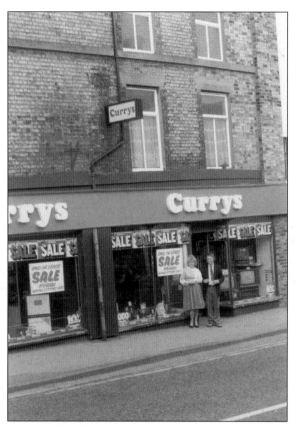

Another national company store, Currys, has closed in Brigg. It had opened in 1927 as mainly a cycle shop, but within a year it was advertising wireless sets and gramophones, as well as cycles, all on 'easy terms made easier'. It prospered, expanded and seemed a permanent fixture, but it became clear it would close when the end of lease signs were displayed in the store's windows. The manager and his wife, Ken and Janet Ayres, stand outside their shop on closing day, Saturday 12 April 1986.

We have chosen to show a rear view of the Corn Exchange not for its eye-catching appeal, but to show some of its positive aspects, the parking space, the solid look of the building and to show its huge size. Plain it may look here but it was so useful to many groups and societies, adults and children alike. After some heated council meetings at Brigg its doors finally closed on 31 May 1992. In 1995 it was demolished.

A rare sight of the old town hall's clock disappearing as it was removed for a good overhaul. The job was given to C. & F. Build Ltd of Haxey. The clock was taken down 19 April 1990 and returned 25 June 1990 as a part of Brigg's regeneration programme.

Dredging of the River Ancholme taking place 13 March 1998 where barges were once a common sight. A major clean up exercise took several weeks to complete. The full length of the old river between Pool End and Coal Dyke End was dredged in order to increase its navigable depth and turn it into a haven for wildlife and an attraction for tourists.

Brigg Fair, Saturday 5 August 1999. This traditional day has had its ups and downs of late but, thanks to a small band of hard workers, the fair has flourished in recent years. It has brought back local fame once more to the town as well as attracting many tourists and stallholders. Can you recognise Grammar School Road?

Whilst the streets were overflowing with visitors and amusements for the Brigg Fair in 1999, the excitement of the day was enough to bring out the television crews in Station Road to put on film Brigg's traditional horse fair. Let's hope it can continue.

Six
Wrawby, Worlaby and Elsham

The crossroads of Wrawby today closely resemble this view of about 1909 when telegraph poles must have been a novelty and when Rose Cottage, centre, was the home of Joe Ashton, a jobbing gardener. The skyline of the cottage and the Black Horse pub behind it remains the same today, although the small building to the left is gone. The church wall was taken down in the 1950s and rebuilt to allow widening of the road on this dangerous corner.

Church Hill, *c.* 1922. A heavily laden vehicle chugs up the hill past the Black Horse on its way out of the village. After a pint at the pub, the locals could get 'one of each' at the fish and chip shop adjoining the white house opposite. Now the house and the little shop are just a memory.

In the mid- to late nineteenth century, Thomas Berridge Carr is listed as the landlord of the Bay Horse in Wrawby, but the same man is in 1882 named as the landlord of the Black Horse. It appears there has been a slight name change. By 1901 Sam Kirk's name appeared above the doorway as in this picture and he stayed until John Braithwaite succeeded him in 1923.

Looking up the incline of Brigg Road into Wrawby, the dominating telegraph poles lead the eyes to George Tong's farm. This card was posted in 1913 before the old Hillside Lodge was altered and enlarged – then it had a fence, now it's a hedge. The three little cottages close by were demolished many years ago.

The opening of the new Primitive Methodist chapel in Wrawby took place on Wednesday 22 February 1913 and must have added considerably to the architectural appearance of the village, being centrally situated. It had accommodation for one hundred worshippers, with seats of pine and windows of glaze glass.It closed over thirty years ago and has been demolished.

In recent years new properties have been built in Vicarage Road where Ashton's gardens used to be, obscuring this view of the old school on the extreme right of the picture. Today, the house in front is privately owned and known as The Lodge, but it was originally the farm foreman's house belonging to College Farm situated across the road.

Wrawby National School, 1897. Perhaps the whole school is posing here for Mr Wilmore, the Brigg photographer, as the school was only built for one hundred and thirty children. We can only surmise the reason for the occasion, it may have been for Queen Victoria's Diamond Jubilee celebrations of that year. Mr William Morris, the head teacher, may be the man to the right in the bowler hat.

Wrawby School in 1951 when Miss Stothard and Miss Bilton were staff and Gus Markham was head. Back row, left to right: Gary Buss, Derek Havercroft, Peter Chapman, Alan Havercroft, Robert Green. Middle row: Clifton Chapman, David Havercroft, John Beveridge, Laurence Stephenson, Brian Green, Terry Pinder, Colin Day, Ivan Betts. Front row: Glenda Driffield, Ann Herrick, Margaret Rose, Ann Latham, Ann Green, Mavis Standerline, Josie Dixon, Irene Andrew, Pat Robinson.

Redholme, the residence of Henry Metcalfe Hett, a Brigg solicitor, in about 1909. This imposing building is situated on Vicarage Road. To the left of the house is a wind pump, used to pump water into a tank in the roof space, providing its own water supply. The property was commandeered by the Army during the last war and is now a retirement home.

A late nineteenth-century view of Vicarage Road, Wrawby, where the thatched cottage, home of the Good family, stands alone with the vicarage beyond, hidden by trees. The first house, built using local bricks, dated from approximately 1856, has stood the test of time but the cottage next door has disappeared, along with those past the shop where the post office stands now.

Tunnel Road in about 1920. A dusty track leads out of the village toward open countryside and Barton Road, a fascinating glimpse into a lost rural setting. Just a few cottages nestle by the roadside, the one nearest Barton Road being occupied by the 'Bakers'. It has since made way for the development of new housing aptly named Bakersfield.

A wonderful picture of a Wrawby butcher, Charles Bett, the proud owner of a Model T Ford, c. 1918. The vehicle probably had a dual purpose; fine for business but with a demountable rear section for the weekend jaunts. It was more than likely assembled at Allen's Brigg coach works.

Wrawby Football Club, 1923. At this time the village team played in Kettleby Lane, opposite the council houses. From left to right, back row: Tom Daubney, Cliff Hocknell, Harry North, -?-, Percy North, Charlie Lusby. Front row: Bob Lidgett, Harry Lidgett, Tommy Elvin, Billy Lidgett, Jim Button, Joe Pigott, -?-, -?-.

This is Low Road, Worlaby. We halt behind a horse and trap opposite the home of greengrocer, Ben Drakes. He lived where the bicycle is propped up and through the archway was his smallholding. On this side all the buildings are now gone, except for the block where the children are playing. This old picture is hard to equate with the same view of today.

White House, Worlaby, 1906. This roof line is just visible on the previous picture of Low Road. These sheep, or rams, on Billy Robinson's lawn (he's in white) are due for selection and transporting, by him, to the Argentine for breeding purposes. A long journey for a young man (b. 1884) but highly profitable if the four or five chosen are the right ones. This house was occupied by the Robinson family as early as 1856.

Top Road, Worlaby, from a postcard sent in 1912 and showing a row of houses that can be recognised today. The small distant shop was in the ownership of Thomas Bradshaw, grocer and draper. He later moved to Main Street to run the post office. The nearest house (now Corner House) belonged to Harry Barnaby, the local vet and farrier.

The church and vicarage, Worlaby, 1913. Today the sign on the gate reads 'Old Vicarage', and Worlaby is now part of a group of five parishes, the vicar residing at Saxby all Saints. This substantial building, now minus the ivy, still stands next to the church of St Clement, which was rebuilt 1873-77 on an ancient site. The Revd George Lewthwaite was the new incumbent in 1911.

Low Road, Worlaby, *c.* 1922. Looking back towards Wrawby and Elsham, the Primitive Methodist chapel is the main feature of this scene. When it closed several decades ago it was given to the village by King's College to be used as a village hall, called College Rooms. It became a very popular place for the locals to enjoy games of whist, etc, until it was demolished in the late 1960s.

All Saints Elsham in a very rural-looking Church Street, *c.* 1908. All the greenery has flourished over the century and the two horse chestnut trees remain, although the gate is gone. The attractive little churchyard looks rather overgrown, yet a haven of peace and tranquillity.

94

New Street, Elsham. This postcard is dated 1908, but the street, or road as locals prefer, has changed very little. At least now the road and paths are neat and tidy and lit. The estate houses on the left look the same as do the cottages in the centre, although a new road, Woodland Drive has been built between them. Among the tall trees beyond is the cricket ground, while across the road two men talk near Baldwin's shop.

The Baldwin family, grocers, were long established in Elsham, having a business there is the 1850s. They also had a cobbler's shop close by in Doll Lane where Ted Etty helped. He let youngsters sit in front of the fire and watch if they behaved themselves. John Baldwin died in 1910 and the grocery was run by his son-in-law, John Etty, seen standing outside the shop with his two small sons, Eric and Tom in 1911.

Chapel Lane, Elsham, in 1925 and the last thatched cottage in the village, where Mr Thorpe, joiner and wheelwright, lived. Beyond the cottage was a sawpit where all the trees from the estate were cut up. Mr Baxter from Church Street was the last person to thatch this property, which was pulled down after the last war. The village hall was eventually erected on the land.

The Wesleyan chapel, Elsham, was situated next to the estate cottages on Chapel Lane and the services were conducted by a minister from the Brigg circuit. It originally had box seats which were later replaced by seats thought to have come from a chapel at Cadney. Mrs Edna Thorpe played the organ during the latter years of its existence. After closure the chapel was used to store potatoes until its demolition in the 1950s.

Maltkiln Lane, Elsham, *c*. 1919. The estate houses on the corner of Chapel Lane are the only clues to the whereabouts of this scene for the old almshouses have been replaced by pensioners' bungalows at Astley Corner. The cottage beyond is gone, where a lady known as Nurse Bontoft once lived with her mother, and where they kept a cow. Sycamore House and Dunn's Paddock complete today's picture.

The Village Minstrels, 18 December, 1930. People from many of Elsham families are seen here at rehearsal in the school rooms. Back row, left to right: G. Wraith, S. Etty, F. Marshall, A. Carpenter, D. Beeston, T. Etty, G. Moody, J. Scott, J. Fidell. Middle row: Mrs Driffill, Mrs Etty, Mrs Short, Mrs Cole, Mrs Holt, Mrs Lingard, Mrs Stow, F. Whitehead. Front row: A. Beeston, J. Norris, G. Bellamy, P. Carline, D. Etty, T. Portess, E. Lingard, C. Cole.

Elsham Show, August 1911. The writer of this card won second prize in this bicycle race at the forty-first show of flowers and sports. These sports were held on the hall's cricket ground beginning at 3.15 p.m. There were open events and others just for estate residents. To the villagers it was the big annual Bank Holiday social function and it brought in six or seven thousand visitors.

Elsham, 1918. A cache of old amateur postcards reveals that young airmen stationed at the aerodrome came here. They wrote brief comments on the back of the cards: 'A.B.F. seated', states the shaking hand, 'Swimming party for Elsham Hall lake'. Decades later these comments were endorsed by retired Wing Commander A.B. Fanstone of Brighton. Sir Francis Astley Corbett generously allowed the airmen free access to all the facilities at the Hall in their spare time.

Seven

Barnetby, Bigby and Cadney cum Howham

G.C. railway station, Barnetby. A wonderful scene of the busy station where three lines from Brigg, Scunthorpe and Lincoln converge and run to the East Coast and the Humber Bank. Today the village station attracts many railway photographers because of the excellent old-fashioned signalling in the area and because of the plentiful rail traffic. This old picture shows the same photographic response taken almost a century ago: such pictures are now so popular. This pre-1912 view of the station's busy activities demonstrates the importance of this railway to Barnetby's development.

The Old Railway crossing, Barnetby. The level crossing keeper's house of Kings Road and the 'pompom' loco provide the backcloth for this group of workers. In 1903 at a parish meeting it was stated that a subway was a necessity as gentlemen with their ponies and traps often had to wait fourteen minutes at the crossing. By January 1913, the building of a subway became a reality, and finally the old crossing was closed – hurray!

Wrawby Junction Box, Barnetby. A dozen railwaymen pose for the cameraman, but the imposing size of the new signalbox tends to make them appear small. The building was constructed in 1916 and is in full use today at this vast intersection of three busy lines. With refurbishment in 2000, the signalmen now have the luxury of an inside loo!

The Station Hotel was the welcoming sight that met travellers on disembarking from their train journeys. The brewers, Hewitt Bros, took over the running of it from the Sutton Bean brewery of Brigg in 1924. Cyril H. Green, the landlord, arrived in 1929, succeeding George Darnell (RAOB). Railway Street is seen to the rear. Times change, and after extensive alterations and modernisation the establishment has a new name – the Whistle and Flute.

The Temperance Hotel was a small hotel in Railway Street close to the station master's house appealing to visitors who preferred a non-alcoholic residence. Near to the railway station and Kings Road, it appears to have been run from about 1909 until the late 1920s by Mrs Prudence Smith. Today it is split into two dwellings, Nos 9 and 11.

Kings Road, Barnetby, *c.* 1911. This part of the road was to be changed considerably with the construction of the subway. Blinds protect the leather goods in Lyne's shop window whilst by the street lamp is Charles Blanchard's tailoring sign. Clearly young children liked William Thorpe's grocery and sweet shop or perhaps they are attracted by the bakery smell at the back of it.

G.A. Lyne and Sons, *c.* 1905. This well known Brigg firm was represented in Barnetby until the First World War. At the Kings Road premises, there was a workshop round the back in the yard where high class saddlery was made and repaired. Locals will recall the building as the post office when Mrs Annie Davis was the postmistress.

From 1880 till 1989 the Railway Inn was in the hands of the Braithwaites. In the 1920s (this picture) it was run by Mr William Needham, son-in-law of William Braithwaite, the previous tenant. Four acres of land accompanied the pub and provided extra income for the publican and his wife. They always kept two cows and sold eggs and butter. In 1929 the Needhams moved nearby to the New Inn at Limber where there was more land and John Braithwaite took over.

'I have put a cross on ma's house, you can see it's nice and open', wrote the sender of this postcard in August 1905. These houses in Silver Street were built by a local man, Mr J.R. Manders, mainly to accommodate workers of the expanding railway network. The view did not remain open for long. Eventually sixty-nine houses were constructed on both sides of the street.

St Barnabas Road in about 1910. A man wheels his cycle past Lowish's milk cart, parked on the corner near West Street. The white house and shop beyond were demolished long ago and the last person to live there was Johnny Howson. John Manders' builders yard is on the left: many years later the site became a petrol station.

Great changes have occurred during the past century in West Street. The white house on the left has gone, as well as virtually all those on the other side, including the double fronted house. Billy Green, one of four butchers in the village, once had his shop here with a slaughterhouse next door. Perhaps the chauffeur driven car belongs to Dr Ffrench.

Queen's Road, Barnetby, 1919. Until 1905, the telegraph had been confined to the railway station. Clearly here, such new facilities still bring out the locals. John Naylor, the postmaster, has his premises far left beyond the telegraph poles, the house now known as Lindum House. Edwin Cuthbert's butchers shop adjoins the ivy-clad house on the right. The thatched cottages were soon to disappear to leave open ground.

Queen's Road, looking back into the village with the post office on the right. On the wall are advertisements for lamp oil, a dyeworks agency and postal facilities. William Howson's grocery is on the corner of West Street. Part of the row of shops cum cottages in St Barnabas Road has been demolished leaving a private residence, No. 60.

Innocent, happy days for children playing in St Barnabas Road outside Mr Yarker's school in 1934 – days when boys wore short trousers and girls wore frocks. Another interesting bygone on this postcard is the pinfold, a brick enclosure for animals, with a gate at the front. An example surviving today can be seen at Scawby.

The staff of Barnetby School pose for what was probably the annual school photograph, with the houses of St Barnabas Road as a background. The staff here were led by Mr George Yarker from Lincoln who had succeeded Mr Edwin Rowe in Autumn 1924 as head. On the back row, second left, is Miss May Freeston and on the front row, left, is Miss Blow, and right, Dora Lusby.

Lord Worsley laid the foundation stone for a new parish church in Barnetby on Monday 19 July 1926. After the ceremony the Bishop of Lincoln, accompanied by local clergy, including Revd M. Greenfield of Limber, who carried the crosier, addressed the large crowd. Ten months later, 10 May 1927, the Bishop returned to consecrate the church to St Barnabas.

Benny's Lane, Barnetby, takes its name from Benny Gooseman who lived in the isolated cottage. Pictured from the top road between Melton Ross and Bigby, Barnetby village can be seen in the distance. It remains a pleasant walk for locals, ending at a field gate in St Barnabas Road.

Main Street, Bigby on a postcard marked 1929 but this picture appears to be from a decade earlier. The farm workers' cottages seem so similar and were owned at that time by the Elwes family. Looking to Barnetby, Lilac Cottage can be seen next to the children and beyond them is Home Farm, recently sold for development.

Bigby rectory, seen here in about 1912, is a fine residence situated on the hillside with magnificent views over the village and countryside beyond. It passed out of the hands of the church long ago and has latterly been owned by British Steel (Corus) and lavishly restored. With the demise of the steel industry it has recently been placed on the property market.

Main Street Howsham. On the reverse of this 1920s postcard is written, 'Day's Row of Houses', seemingly the family living here at Appletree Cottage at the time. Next door, at the present No. 19 Joiners Cottage is a board advertising C.H. Thompson, probably the local carpenter of the village.

This postcard, posted in 1905, shows the now redundant Primitive Methodist chapel, recently converted into a home, in Main Street Howsham. Built in 1838 and restored in 1883 it remains outwardly very similar today. The three pairs of cottages are still there as is the house beyond the tree. There are now telegraph poles on either side of the road, but still only one footpath.

The Wesleyan chapel, Howsham which is the present day Cadney cum Howsham village hall, looking very much today as on this old card, although the gate and the chimney are gone. A foundation stone dates the chapel to 14 August 1832. 'The Firs' on the right remains recognisable, as does the stable block beyond. The narrow road leads westwards toward Cadney, two miles away.

Grayson Clarke, the Brigg photographer, took pictures of different parts of Cadney All Saints church when restoration work was being carried out. The ancient building had been closed for many years after it was allowed to get into a dilapidated condition. The roof had fallen in at various places, while the floor and seating were almost beyond repair. The Revd Dr Hicks, Bishop of Lincoln, was instrumental in a movement being set up to completely restore one of the most interesting churches in the district. He performed the opening ceremony 4 June 1913.

Eight

Scawby, Hibaldstow and Broughton

Scawby Road, Brigg, 1913. The gentle pace of North Lincolnshire life is portrayed here in this scene of horse-drawn traffic both leaving and entering Brigg by Victoria Cottages. The horses and traps coming into the town are about to pass the slower horse and cart of Henry Chapman. He lived at No. 12 West Terrace and was a coal dealer for many years and into the 1930s.

Scawby Road, Brigg, from a postcard sent in 1935 by a youngster, Joan, stating that her house is further up the road. The two houses on the corner of Silversides Lane and Scawby Road had been built in the early 1930s by the Brigg firm of R.M. Phillips. This view today, officially known as Scawby Brook, looks very similar, although everything is a little more mature.

Mill Place, Brigg, c. 1907. A rare picture taken by W.B. Robinson, illustrating a time when these impressive properties were the homes of the middle classes, mostly business people with interests in Brigg. The tower mill behind, belonging to millers, John and Alfred Bratley, once a landmark, has gone, as has the Scawby milestone informing travellers it is one mile to Brigg.

The Old Pinfold, Scawby, 1911. Often originally situated on the edge of villages, these enclosures for stray animals have now generally fallen into decay. Scawby's was no exception, but thankfully the parish council restored the remains in the 1970s. Now lacking its door, this vestige of another age still stands on Brigg Road.

The village pond, c. 1909. A winter's day, the trees devoid of their leaves and summer seeming a long way off as village children pose by the pond. They appear well dressed, each boy sporting a white celluloid collar and the customary cap. Their headmaster, Mr John Whittaker, lives in the centre house directly behind them.

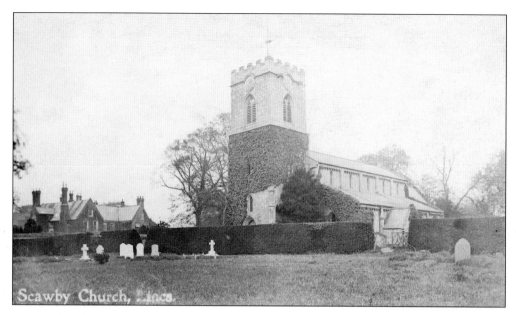

Scawby church is dedicated to St Hybald and built of limestone from local quarries. It fell into a state of disrepair and was rebuilt in around 1840, with the exception of the medieval tower, and the cost was borne by the parishioners. Close by stands the seventeenth-century hall constructed of red brick by Richard Nelthorpe. The church contains many memorials to the Nelthorpe family.

Scawby Hall photographed by Richard Neal Lister from Hull in 1906. He took many pictures of the village in the early twentieth century, including interior views of the hall. The magnificent drawing room contains some fine furniture and paintings. Above the fireplace is a painting by George Stubbs of Sir Henry Nelthorpe and his second wife Elizabeth. Robert N. Sutton Nelthorpe was lord of the manor at this time.

Oglesby's shop in Scawby, c. 1905. John Oglesby had recently taken over the business from George Hooton, shopkeeper and watchmaker. He had been here since about 1860. In 1905 John Oglesby, the grocer, was also a coal dealer. The building looks different today due to alterations in 1935. The family name is still over the shop window, and the wall to the extreme left, next to the Sutton Arms public house, still remains.

Infant School, Scawby, c. 1920. The village seems to have been well off with two schools close to the church. To the left here is the one for older children and the other, built in 1901, is for infants and stands on the opposite side of the road. At this time Miss Mabel Bell was the infant mistress.

Will Tutty sold and repaired cycles and motorbikes at his premises on Messingham Lane, almost opposite where St Martins Road is today. Much later he ran a local taxi service until about 1957. By his side in this picture, from about 1935, is his daughter Joan's friend, Joan Button. His cottage on the left was pulled down thirty years ago.

Scawby Gull Ponds. Blackheaded gulls came to breed each year in the two lakes just outside Scawby village at Twigmoor. During the Second World War, Canadian soldiers, billeted in the surrounding woods, frightened the birds away and they never returned. This species of gull had nested here for at least one hundred years and could only be found at two other sites.

Vicarage Lane, Scawby, 1910. Scawby remains an attractive village today due to the retention of so many of its old buildings. Entering the village from Broughton, the white washed estate cottages just beyond Scawby Hall Lodge have unfortunately not survived, but the wall to the hall gardens remains unchanged.

West Street, Scawby, 1912. This part of the road from Sturton was then known as Station Road. The stone house belonged to Joseph Cliff who lived at the Grove opposite and consisted of two dwellings for his employees. It was demolished in the early 1960s to make way for a new road, and housing development called Beechwood Drive. The cottages closer to the village centre have been preserved.

Sturton post office, 1905. Harrison Butler was the sub-postmaster and licensed dealer in tea and tobacco at the general store housed in the first building. The rooms of the adjoining cottage were sunk three or four feet below pavement level and this property, dating from the seventeenth century, has now been demolished. Main Street is to the right and the road leads to the station.

Scawby and Hibaldstow station. The complete staff of workers, led by stationmaster John Fowler, pose for Mr Lister on this postcard view from about 1906. The station opened on 2 April 1849, simultaneously with the others on the line between Gainsborough and Brigg, it being a mile and a half from Scawby village, while Hibaldstow lay much nearer. These buildings, including the goods yard, were on the north side of the line to Brigg.

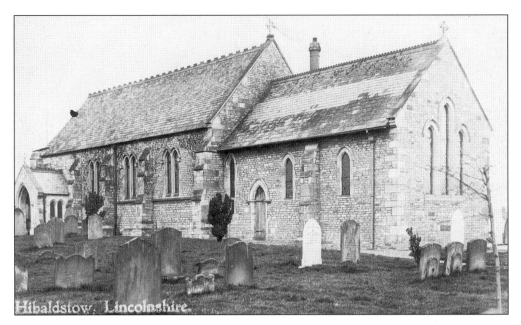

St Hibald's church, Hibaldstow, photographed from the south side, *c.* 1906. This early building is interesting as its original tower fell in July 1875 after the old nave had been taken down. A new nave was constructed 1876/77 but lack of funds prohibited the rebuilding of a tower until 1958. The chimney seen here was for the heating system of the church.

Church Street, Hibaldstow, *c.* 1907. Today large trees partially hide the new tower of St Hibald's visible in this view. The house to the left is still to be seen, along with recent developments between it and Ford Lane. Richard Skaith was the local carpenter, undertaker and wheelwright. The only buildings remaining on this side are the grocer's shop and the brick house beyond.

119

The Wheatsheaf Hotel, Hibaldstow. The cottages and milestone informing travellers that it's 19 miles to Lincoln may have gone, but the hotel lives on. The photographer, standing in the field where the annual fair is held, aims his camera at David Jones' pub, landlord prior to the Great War. The hotel was advertised for anglers as only ten minutes walk to the River Ancholme.

Manor House, Hibaldstow, 1906. The roof line of the house is visible in the previous picture, facing Station Road. There was an earlier building on this site where the East family farmed the land at Manor Farm for much of the nineteenth century. This substantial brick building was built to replace it in 1893, when it was occupied by George Trafford.

West Street, Hibaldstow, 1909. Manchester House still stands on the corner of Cockett's Lane and West Street, but Edward Cockett's grocers shop next door has gone. Established in the previous century, this family business was later taken over by the Gilberts, and during the Second World War the premises became the Home Guard headquarters. Isaac Barnett's post office and shop on Redbourne Road is now Dixon's news agency.

East Street, Hibaldstow, in an early postcard view taken almost a hundred years ago, but remarkably unchanged today. The United Free Methodist chapel, dating from 1865, remains active, with Bayes Villa built into the space between it and the still present cottages and there is a pavement now. Beechwood Farm House, now a listed building, appears here to be receiving visitors at the door.

This is the front of Beckwater House and our mill and house in the distance', writes William Andrew on this postcard view of Barnside, Hibaldstowe on 7 August 1912. The mill was demolished in about 1920 but the mill house survives. Thomas Allison's house at No. 21 Beckside remains, along with Rose Cottage nearby. The large barn on the left at Brookhouse Farm, is now derelict and the adjoining farmhouse long gone.

Beckside, Hibaldstow, 1905. A postcard from grandma's album features the house and smallholding of the Tuxford family. As well as working the land, they kept a cow or two, and had a $\frac{3}{4}$ acre grass paddock close to Northfield Mill. Alfred Reeson was the miller here. The young boy with the baby and perambulator complete this nostalgic view by the old mill stream.

Scunthorpe Road, Broughton, 1906. Not the expected name of High Street today, but instantly recognisable by the village pond and the well-preserved Saxon church. The cottages were pulled down around 1960 as structurally unsound. Cigarettes and sweets were sold at the little wooden shop beyond by Mr 'Goodie' Lamming, followed by Mr Marshall who was very generous to servicemen during the last war.

High Street, Broughton. Not a common postcard view of a village, but a formidable group of workmen standing stretched across the street. The writer dated the card 11 May 1909, and explains, 'The men all commence work on Monday next' – but what work, and where? 'They have all been busy with the tennis court'.

Ye Olde Thatch Broughton, 1907. Above the doorway is a large Tadcaster Tower Brewery sign and above that the publican's name, John William Ayre, landlord of the inn for over thirty years. The photographer is standing in the yard through which locals flocked, leading to Thatch Field where Smith and Warren's fair was held. Beyond the gateway the house in Chapel Lane can just be seen.

High Street, Broughton. Another part of the village to have vanished is Ayre's shop which stood almost opposite the Thatch Inn. Old enamel signs adorn the side of the building and a fading sign to the left of the window reads F. Ayre, carrier. They sold almost everything at this little general store which was converted into a fish and chip shop before its demise.

'Bon Accord', High Street, Broughton, the home of John Nixon, threshing machine owner, on the corner of Beck Lane helps to place this scene, as does the end of the Wesleyan chapel. On that side, the white cottage has disappeared. By the quaint wooden street sign, the children face the camera at the corner of Village Farm, now Wells Court.

High Street, Broughton, 1906. The same street sign as in the previous photograph, only the photographer is standing at the corner of Village Farm. The row of houses on the left stand as steadfast today, but those on the right have disappeared, one by one, now none remain.

Broughton in 1906. Such old views of a familiar village can sometimes be difficult to fathom – where was this taken from? Where is the church? Perhaps the washing line leading to No. 6 Appleby Lane helps understanding, or No. 4 shown above the clothes, maybe the large roof of the Dog and Rat? Can you spot the white cottage shown in the next picture?

High Street, Broughton, 1920. To stand on the roundabout by the Dog and Rat today would be reckless, but that is the position where the cameraman stood to take this view of the narrow dirt road leading to the church. The street here has been widened appreciably, but Clock House on the left and the opposite white cottage of Newmans remain today, although fine bungalows have replaced the further similar limestone dwellings.

Chapel Lane, Broughton, c. 1930. High hedges, brick walls and no pavements continue to be part of this unchanging scene, although the narrow lane is now tarmacked. On this postcard the Primitive chapel is just out of sight opposite the now charming and most photographable cottage seen further down Chapel Road called Sunnyside Cottage.

Primitive Methodist Chapel, Broughton, 1913. This impressive stone building constructed in 1841 had an upstairs with a balcony all round with beautiful woodwork and an organ which was pumped by hand. On the ground floor, at the side of the chapel, the schoolrooms could be found. Following the amalgamation of the Primitive and Wesleyan congregations, this lovely building was sold, eventually pulled down and a bungalow built, using some of the stone.

Brooklands, Broughton, *c.* 1930. The church tower has been a favourite vantage point for photographers. This picture shows the beginning of Broughton's urbanization, with houses newly built by Harry Goates, landlord of the Red Lion, all known then as Harry's Dream. In contrast, Manor Farm is one of the oldest buildings in Broughton.

Bridge Road, Wressle, on a postcard from Jesse Skinner at Dairy Farm in December 1941, sending 'Best wishes for a happy Christmas, and for Victory 1942'. The farmhouse has been demolished and replaced by a bungalow built away from the road and tall trees. The large shed remains and the Wells family, the present owners, have seen the monkey tree in the field grow to huge proportions.